PRAYERS

God Always Answers

For Blessings

Publications International, Ltd.

INTRODUCTION

Prayer is a special opportunity for each of us to build a personal relationship with God: to move from the one-to-many feeling of reading Scripture into a one-on-one dialogue. We can ask questions, share our concerns, and confess our lower moments. But even the most "model Christian" can sometimes feel like these prayers go unheard — not because God isn't listening, but because we can't see or don't understand the answer we receive.

Every good gift and every perfect gift is from above, and cometh down from the Father of lights, with whom is no variableness, neither shadow of turning.
— *James 1:17*

The Bible is filled with God's promises to bless his people in myriad ways, but this verse from James also points out God's consistency. When you pray, you always receive an answer, even if the answer is for you to be patient or a simple "no." With thought, reflection, and review of Scripture, you can learn to pray more effectively and see God's answers more clearly. Be the most consistent worshiper you can be, and approach God with the same methodical attention he gives to you.

And God said, This is the token of the covenant which I make between me and you and every living creature that is with you, for perpetual generations: I do set my bow in the cloud, and it shall be for a token of a covenant between me and the earth.

— Genesis 9:12-13

In the dead of winter, God of springtimes, I'm gardening. Carrot tops rooting, sweet potatoes vining. I don't doubt the outcome since I've learned at your knee to live as if. As if useless can become useful; as if seemingly dead can live; as if spring will come. How does a winter garden grow? With hope, knowing that you, O God, color even our wintry days from love's spring palette.

*T*hat the communication of thy faith may become effectual by the acknowledging of every good thing which is in you in Christ Jesus.

— Philemon 1:6

Blessings upon you. The blessing of perfect acceptance in the face of daunting circumstances. The blessing of contentment and peace while the winds blow and the waves rise higher and higher. The blessing of knowing when acceptance must turn to action for the sake of all concerned. The blessing of strength to forsake contentment and peace for the purpose of comforting another. The blessing of discernment: to recognize when to wait, and to understand when to move.

*F or every creature of God is good,
and nothing to be refused, if it be
received with thanksgiving: For it is
sanctified by the word of God and prayer.*

— *1 Timothy 4:4-5*

Lord, being in love is a magical gift.
Everything seems brighter and sharper in
focus. My heart soars and my spirit is light as
air, and all because of the love of another. But
help me to also seek that deeper, more lasting
love that comes from truly knowing another,
even when the fires of passion become a gentle
and steady simmer. Let love always be in my
life, no matter what form it comes in. Love of
any kind is a magical gift. Thank you, Lord.

T he Lord is thy keeper: the Lord is
thy shade upon thy right hand.
The sun shall not smite thee by day,
nor the moon by night.

— Psalm 121:5-6

Lord, let my light shine brightly, even if it
makes me feel uncomfortable. I am not used
to standing in the spotlight. But you have
convinced me that there is nothing wrong with
feeling the love of who I am in your eyes, so
help me get over the feeling of embarrassment
and let my talents and gifts reveal themselves.
There is no pride in letting the lamp of love
you have lit within me give forth its glorious
light. Show me how to enlighten the world
and yet stay humble and grateful and true.

Rejoice evermore. Pray without ceasing. In every thing give thanks: for this is the will of God in Christ Jesus concerning you.

— *1 Thessalonians 5:16–18*

God, the blessed feeling of being at home in your loving presence is like nothing else. The joy I feel when I know I never walk alone is the greatest of gifts, and when I look around at the wonderful people you have chosen to walk with me through life — my family and my friends — I truly know that I am loved. Thank you, God, for these miracles, these blessings, far too numerous to count. And to think I never have to look too far from home to find them is the best miracle of all.

N ay, in all these things we are more than conquerors through him that loved us.

— *Romans 8:37*

Lord, I'm looking forward to this new phase of my life. It is full of promise and hope, though I know that challenges will surely come as well. I know you have all the courage, strength, faithfulness, and love I need to meet each moment from a perspective of peace. I just need to stay tethered to you in prayer, listening for your Spirit to guide me and turn my thoughts continually back toward you. That's the key to a good life.

B e ye mindful always of his covenant; the word which he commanded to a thousand generations.

— 1 Chronicles 16:15

May you know that a wisdom and a love transcend the things you will see and touch today. Walk in this light each step of the way. Never forget that there is more to this existence than the material side of things. And be blessed when you suddenly become aware of it: in the smile of a child, in the recognition of your own soul's existence, in the dread of death, and in the longing for immortality.

Happy is he that hath the God of Jacob for his help, whose hope is in the Lord his God: Which made heaven, and earth, the sea, and all that therein is: which keepeth truth for ever.

— *Psalm 146:5–6*

Bless our work, Lord of vineyards and seas. We yearn to be connected with what we do and to do something that matters. Show us that what we do is as indelible as a handprint on fresh concrete even though our mark may be in spots no one can see right now except us. Bless our left-behind marks, for with you as our foundation, our work is as essential to the overall structure of life as a concrete pillar.

A nd when they had prayed, the place was shaken where they were assembled together; and they were all filled with the Holy Ghost, and they spake the word of God with boldness.

— Acts 4:31

There are days when we feel confident, assured, and emboldened. It's tempting to say, "This is my lucky day!" But with God, every day is lucky, and there's no luck involved. He emboldens us. We reach for him and he gives us strength.

A nd I will cleanse them from all their iniquity, whereby they have sinned against me; and I will pardon all their iniquities, whereby they have sinned, and whereby they have transgressed against me.

— *Jeremiah 33:8*

How can we put others' mistakes in perspective? God not only forgives the sin but understands the heart of the sinner. We tiny mortals can try to do the same! True forgiveness brings us closer to God, which is the greatest blessing.

T hus saith the Lord of hosts; If thou wilt walk in my ways, and if thou wilt keep my charge, then thou shalt also judge my house, and shalt also keep my courts, and I will give thee places to walk among these that stand by.

— *Zechariah 3:7*

Walking is a great metaphor throughout the Bible. Our choices affect our own steps and the quality of the path we take. How have you tried to improve your path? Who walks beside you in God's ways?

A nd it came to pass, that, as he was praying in a certain place, when he ceased, one of his disciples said unto him, Lord, teach us to pray.

— *Luke 11:1*

Think of life as a long series of opportunities to set a good example for others. To love your neighbor as you love yourself includes sharing your best "trade secrets" for anyone to use. The disciples watched Jesus in private prayer and reflection and asked him to be a role model for them.

F or there are three that bear record in heaven, the Father, the Word, and the Holy Ghost: and these three are one.

— 1 John 5:7

Were there skeptics in your childhood math classes who asked questions like, "How can infinity plus one still be infinity?" The fact of the Trinity is a cause for awe and wonder, not skepticism.

T hen saith he unto his disciples,
The harvest truly is plenteous, but
the labourers are few; Pray ye therefore
the Lord of the harvest, that he will send
forth labourers into his harvest.

— Matthew 9:37–38

Here Jesus Christ calls for more religious
"labourers" to help him preach to the growing
crowds of believers. With too much to do and
not enough help, our "harvests," whatever
they may be, can also wither in the fields. But
when we bring together our community, we
harvest our abundance — more than enough
to share with others.

E paphras, who is one of you, a servant of Christ, saluteth you, always labouring fervently for you in prayers, that ye may stand perfect and complete in all the will of God.

— Colossians 4:12

All we really know about Epaphras is that Paul shared Epaphras's kind words in a handful of his epistles. It's lovely to think about a network of very early believers who cared so much for one another's beliefs and salvation. They were loving and courageous in a time when it endangered their lives.

*A*nd it came to pass in those days, that he went out into a mountain to pray, and continued all night in prayer to God.

— Luke 6:12

Solitude can be the best spiritual medium. People have always been moved to pray by the beauty and sheer scale of the outdoors, surrounded by God's creation.

*P*rayer has been hedged about with too many man-made rules. I am convinced that God has intended prayer to be as simple and natural, and as constant a part of our spiritual life, as the intercourse between a child and his parent in the home.

— Rosalind Goforth

*B*ut know that the Lord hath set apart him that is godly for himself: the Lord will hear when I call unto him.

— Psalms 4:3

Psalm 4 shows confident prayer in action. God's power is awesome, and the fear of God helps to create the reverence with which we pray to him for help.

W ith my whole heart have I
sought thee: O let me not
wander from thy commandments.
Thy word have I hid in mine heart,
that I might not sin against thee.

— *Psalms* 119:10–11

Practice makes perfect, especially with God.
If someone asked, could you list the ten
commandments, or explain the context of one
of his miracles in the Gospel of John? We
often memorize frivolous things without
meaning to. Perhaps that energy can be
redirected into stoking our love for God.

*A*nd *the Lord appeared to Solomon by night, and said unto him, I have heard thy prayer.*

— 2 Chronicles 7:12

King Solomon built a temple and prayed for God to bless it with his presence. God chose to favor the temple as a place for worship, putting a sacred space in the center of a group of believers. Chances are good that your church is still part of the social backbone of your community.

*T*hou hast beset me behind and before, and laid thine hand upon me. Such knowledge is too wonderful for me; it is high, I cannot attain unto it.

— Psalms 139:5–6

"Amazing Grace" compares finding God to moving from blindness to sight, but the distance is just as great from our own sight to God's.

And they continued stedfastly in the apostles' doctrine and fellowship, and in breaking of bread, and in prayers.

— Acts 2:42

Picture a church, anywhere in the world, anytime since the dawn of Christianity. Details of worship vary over time, but the basics are the same as they always have been. Believers can share Scripture and prayer and good works in one pipeline that lasts for millennia.

And they sing the song of Moses the servant of God, and the song of the Lamb, saying, Great and marvellous are thy works, Lord God Almighty; just and true are thy ways, thou King of saints.

— *Revelation 15:3*

I felt enchantment when my angel brushed my face with silken fingers. I felt empowered when my angel whispered forgiveness to my soul. I felt protected when my angel offered me shelter and lightness beneath her wings. I felt enlightened when my angel showed me how to reach for my dreams among the stars. In the Lord's flock I find strength and comfort.

*T*herefore all things whatsoever ye would that men should do to you, do ye even so to them: for this is the law and the prophets.

— Matthew 7:12

We are given our lights to let them shine, not to hide them or fear our pride. There is a godly way to express every talent and a charitable outlet for every gift! When we open our storehouse of talents and treasures, the whole world benefits and is made brighter by generous loving kindness. We honor God through our willingness to share with and enrich others.

F or the fruit of the Spirit is in all goodness and righteousness and truth.

— *Ephesians 5:9*

The mind is like a garden of fertile soil into which the seeds of our ideas and intentions are planted. With love and nurture, those seeds bloom forth to manifest in our lives as wonderful opportunities and events. Lord, please help me to plant fruitful seeds of goodness and light in my own life and those around me.

B ut let it be the hidden man of the heart, in that which is not corruptible, even the ornament of a meek and quiet spirit, which is in the sight of God of great price.

—1 Peter 3:4

The seasons have meaning with our quiet loved ones. In spring, we weed the beds and plant the flowers. In fall, we pick the peaches, apples, and berries. In winter, we bundle up in afghans before the fire, reading, sharing, and laughing, with bellies full of warming meals. When spring returns, daffodil bulbs poke up their shoots through softening earth. As we work together and nurture one another, our love grows.

T herefore take no thought, saying, What shall we eat? or, What shall we drink? or, Wherewithal shall we be clothed? But seek ye first the kingdom of God, and his righteousness; and all these things shall be added unto you.

— *Matthew 6:31,33*

By investing in yourself with faith and works, you improve your present and your future. So go ahead — volunteer to teach classes, take that mission trip, join a Bible study. Consult faith in your heart as you make choices with your life and your time and your way will be illuminated.

A farmer prayed for some deciding hint in his choice of seed for his land. On his way home he held a bundle in his lap which was in a newspaper wrapper. In one column on the wrapper directly under his eyes was an article on the soils and products of his country which opened his vision and made his farming safe and profitable.

— Russell H. Conwell

B ut Jesus said, Suffer little children, and forbid them not, to come unto me: for of such is the kingdom of heaven.

— Matthew 19:14

Our hearts are glad when we see a new child for the first time, whether our own or those of our loved ones. We smile toward a distant destination in our minds. We bend to them, reaching a finger toward their miraculously tiny hands, their downy hair, all these hallmarks of God's creation. Thank you, Lord, for our beautiful children, challenging and vibrant in your image.

Some people seem to regard prayer as the rehearsal of a set form of solemn words, learned largely from the Bible or a liturgy; and when uttered they are only from the throat outward. Genuine prayer is a believing soul's direct converse with God. Phillips Brooks has condensed it into four words—a "true wish sent Godward."

— Theodore L. Cuyler, D.D.

B less the Lord, ye his angels, that excel in strength, that do his commandments, hearkening unto the voice of his word.

— *Psalm 103:20*

God, I couldn't help noticing all the loveliness you placed in the world today! This morning I saw a sunrise that made my heart beat faster. I watched a father gently help his child across a busy parking lot; his tenderness was much like yours. I spied an elderly couple sitting on a bench. As the man told jokes, their laughter lifted my spirits. Later, I talked with a friend who aids needy families; her compassion inspired me. Thank you, Lord, for everything that is beautiful and good in the world.

*S*et your affection on things above,
not on things on the earth.

— *Colossians 3:2*

There is no greater mystery than love, Lord
of covenants and promises. We are especially
in its presence on an anniversary. Bless those
who live, day after day after ordinary day,
within the fullness of lifelong love, surely
one of life's greatest mysteries. Bless them
as they honor their past, even while they
create a future. Let us bow before their
accomplishments, which are an inspiration and
blessing to us all.

Our Lord taught us to pray in secret, in simplicity, with the eye on God alone, in humility, in the spirit of forgiving love. But the chief truth He reiterated was ever this: to pray in faith. And He defined that faith, not only as a trust in God's goodness or power, but as the definite assurance that we have received the very thing we ask.

— Rev. Andrew Murray

H erein is my Father glorified, that ye bear much fruit; so shall ye be my disciples.

— John 15:8

The surge of adrenaline as we look over our shoulders to see who's gaining on us is as natural as breathing, Lord, and we pick up the pace to keep ahead. Competition is exhilarating, and we welcome its challenges. Yet, competition out of control creates bare-knuckle conflict within us, and we are shocked at the lengths to which we will go to win. We must look ahead to you, not backward to those we're "besting."

About devotional feelings, about religious observances, however excellent and blessed, we may deceive ourselves; for we may put them in the place of sanctification, of righteousness and true holiness. About justice and honesty we cannot deceive ourselves; for they are sanctification itself, righteousness itself, true holiness itself, the very likeness of God, and the very grace of God.

— Charles Kingsley

I exhort therefore, that, first of all, supplications, prayers, intercessions, and giving of thanks, be made for all men; For kings, and for all that are in authority; that we may lead a quiet and peaceable life in all godliness and honesty.

—1 Timothy 2:1–2

Life is full of trade-offs, Lord, and I need to make one. Guide my search for a career where I can have both a life and a living. Your balance is not found running in a circle, but along a beckoning path where enough is more than sufficient; where money comes second to family, community, and self; where success takes on new meaning; and where, in the giving up, I gain wealth beyond belief.

And so it may come to pass in later life that our specific petitions for this or that thing may grow fewer. To put it another way—the petitions are fewer because the prayer is deeper and truer.

— W. Boyd Carpenter, D.D.

*T*ake therefore no thought for the morrow: for the morrow shall take thought for the things of itself. Sufficient unto the day is the evil thereof.

— Matthew 6:34

God, so much of life is fleeting. It seems like we are always saying goodbye to this person or that situation. But there is one thing we can always count on—your love. Like the foundation upon which our lives are built, your love gives us stability, something to hold onto when everything around us is whirling chaos. Like the roof over our heads, your love shelters us from life's worst storms. Thank you, God, for your everlasting love.

*A*nd I will strengthen them in the Lord; and they shall walk up and down in his name, saith the Lord.

— *Zechariah 10:12*

✠ ✠ ✠

How has God's strength shown itself in your life? Do you ask for God's help when you need it?

*I*t is the very nature of love to give up and forget itself for the sake of others. It takes their needs and makes them its own, it finds its real joy in living and dying for others.

— *Rev. Andrew Murray*

B rethren, I count not myself to have apprehended: but this one thing I do, forgetting those things which are behind, and reaching forth unto those things which are before, I press toward the mark for the prize of the high calling of God in Christ Jesus.

— *Philippians 3:13–14*

☩ ☩ ☩

It can be tempting to write hope off as weak. We often hear expressions like "I hope it doesn't rain," where hope is an idle wish. But hope matters! Hope, love, and faith are closely related. They are the inseparable sister virtues, each one stronger through association with the other two. When used together, these beautiful qualities multiply their power and result in immense strength. We persevere in the Lord with this strength!

While it may be difficult for a human father to discern between the motives of his child who brings him a gift so as to be sure that the gift is the exhibition of a pure affection, yet the Lord has no such limitation. He knows whether the offering is a gambling venture or a lovely deed inspired by a pure, unselfish love.

— Russell H. Conwell

T he Lord thy God shall bless thee in all thy works, and in all that thou puttest thine hand unto.

— Deuteronomy 15:10

Bless this candle-lit festival of birthday celebration, Lord, for our special loved one. Join us as we blow out candles and joke about setting the cake ablaze, about golden ages and silver hairs. Our laughter is bubbling up from gratitude that the years are only enriching this special celebrant. We are grateful that the years are also enriching our lives as friends and family as well, for we are the ones receiving the best birthday gift today: the gift of knowing this special person. Thank you for sharing.

I have called upon thee, for thou wilt hear me, O God: incline thine ear unto me, and hear my speech.

— Psalms 17:6

*A*nd let us not be weary in well doing: for in due season we shall reap, if we faint not.

— *Galatians 6:9*

May you be the leader you were meant to be today. May you find courage to temper your business goals with an eye toward human compassion. May you carefully weigh the consequences of every tough decision you make—the impact on those around you. May you know that one greater than you goes before you and stands behind you, offering great wisdom.

He will breathe His own life, which is all prayer, into us.

— Henry Altemus

Bless the Lord, ye his angels, that excel in strength, that do his commandments, hearkening unto the voice of his word.

— Psalm 103:20

Dear Lord, sometimes our coworkers feel like family and we are grateful to belong. We do our finest work under the boosted morale of a warm and creative workgroup. Bless the folks down the hall, across the room, in the next department, or in the office next door. They are more than coworkers, they are workday neighbors.

P ray on, dear one—the power lies that way.

— Mary Slessor

I am the good shepherd, and know my sheep, and am known of mine.

— John 10:14

Our parents are wonderful; they are kids at heart. They tag along as we explore, hold the shells and "pretty rocks" we just have to keep, tell us jokes and laugh with us. They sing us to sleep on hot summer nights and hold our hands as we walk unsteady paths. Bless our parents now and forever.

B egin by setting apart some time every day, say ten or fifteen minutes, in which you say to God and to yourself, that you come to Him now [to pray] for others. Let it be after your morning or evening prayer, or any other time. If you cannot secure the same time every day, be not troubled. Only see that you do your work.

— Rev. Andrew Murray

There may be ten thousand dreams which are of no special value and which are caused by natural law. But God seems to use only one here and there for his special purposes. Thousands of seeds fall on the earth, but only one may be selected to grow.

— Russell H. Conwell

W herefore I put thee in remembrance that thou stir up the gift of God, which is in thee by the putting on of my hands. For God hath not given us the spirit of fear; but of power, and of love, and of a sound mind.

—2 Timothy 1:6–7

Exercise is so good. I lace up my shoes and feel my engaging muscles sing your praises— you made this warm machine that I must mindfully care for. I will pray now, with energy, exertion, gutting it out. But I will not pray with words for a while. You are here as I pick up speed. And what, after all, needs to be said aloud at this moment? How better to honor you than to use the incredible tools you've given us?

new heart also will I give you, and a new spirit will I put within you: and I will take away the stony heart out of your flesh, and I will give you an heart of flesh.

— Ezekiel 36:26

My heart is at home. Where better to think of you, Lord, than at home? It is where we have our history, begin our traditions, take our rites of passage. It is where we are first loved, first safe, first found to be special. It is where we are sheltered and nourished, then equipped and sent on our way. Throughout it all, you sit invisibly in our midst, blessing our spaces. Help us to always see the beauty, the opportunities in them. Bless us, the homebodies.

A little tot prayed for a "singing doll," and her mother told her that a doll was too small a matter to pray for. But the father overheard the conversation, and, after purchasing the most costly one he could find at his noon hour, he left it on the little one's bed in the night when everyone else was supposed to be asleep.

— Russell H. Conwell

W hat? know ye not that your body is the temple of the Holy Ghost which is in you, which ye have of God, and ye are not your own? For ye are bought with a price: therefore glorify God in your body, and in your spirit, which are God's.

— 1 Corinthians 6:19–20

T hat God can give blessing, without the use of the ordinary means, on man's part, there is no question. That he has done so is a matter of record. Yet we should remember that there were but two miraculous draughts of fishes, and only twice did our Lord make bread without the use of seed-time, harvest, grinding and baking.

— D.W. Whittle

The heavens declare the glory of God; and the firmament sheweth his handywork. Day unto day uttereth speech, and night unto night sheweth knowledge. There is no speech nor language, where their voice is not heard. Their line is gone out through all the earth, and their words to the end of the world.

— Psalm 19:1–4

Bless the soil beneath our feet and the sky overhead, and make us one with it. We are catching on, catching up with ourselves, creator God, and catching a glimpse of the fading streams and trash-strewn seas we have long ignored. Bless and use our reclamation efforts, for it is a task we can't accomplish alone. With your help, we can bind up and reclaim this poor old earth. We feel whispers of hope in the winds of changed hearts and minds. We are grateful for another chance.

A master cares for the food of his servant, a general of his soldiers, a father of his child. And will not the Father in heaven care for the child who has in prayer given himself up to His interests? We may indeed in full confidence say: Father, I live for Thy honor and Thy work; I know Thou carest for me.

— Henry Altemus

H atred stirreth up strifes: but love covereth all sins.

— Proverbs 10:12

Bless this gathering of what, at first glance, looks like mismatched parts, encircling God, for we want to become a family. Guide us as we step closer to one another, but not so close as to crowd. Heal wounds from past events that made this union possible. Bless the children with the courage to try new relatives, new traditions, new homes. Step closer, loving God, and lead us.

G od is love, and he loves the lover. His intrinsic nature compels him to answer the call of his beloved.

— Russell H. Conwell

I am the vine, ye are the branches: He that abideth in me, and I in him, the same bringeth forth much fruit: for without me ye can do nothing.

— John 15:5

With God, you have everything — without God, you have nothing. The contrast is stark and effective. All good things must come through a relationship with God. If they don't, then they're not truly good — buyer beware.

*J*esus assures us that secret prayer cannot be fruitless: its blessing will show itself in our life. We have but in secret, alone with God, to entrust our life before men to Him; He will reward us openly; He will see to it that the answer to prayer be made manifest in His blessing upon us.

— Henry Altemus

I thank my God, making mention of thee always in my prayers.

— Philemon 4

Heartfelt prayer on someone else's behalf is a great reason to talk to God, and it can also give you a spiritual boost. To love your neighbor as yourself includes praying for their well being!

We may always pray to be made better men. We may always pray to be made wiser men. These prayers will always be answered; for they are prayers for the very Spirit of God himself, from whom comes all goodness and all wisdom.

— Charles Kingsley

N ow I beseech you, brethren, for the Lord Jesus Christ's sake, and for the love of the Spirit, that ye strive together with me in your prayers to God for me.

— *Romans 15:30*

Paul reached out to communities around the known world and took care to treat each one with the utmost love and respect. His epistle to the Romans is often called his masterpiece, and in its conclusion we find this request for prayer. Paul wrote much of the New Testament yet still understood the great need for community and a shared conversation with God among all his followers.

W e form our expectations: they take shape from our poor little limited surroundings; but the prayer in its spirit may be wider than we imagine. To answer it according to our expectations might be not to answer it truly.

— W. Boyd Carpenter, D.D.

I n all thy ways acknowledge him, and he shall direct thy paths.

— Proverbs 3:6

One reason the Lord's Prayer is so powerful is that it does acknowledge God's power in many ways. As we say it, we feel the reverence we owe to God, and we can humbly ask for his guidance.

When you cannot find words,
when your words appear cold
and feeble, just believe: The Holy Spirit
is praying in me. Be quiet before God,
and give Him time and opportunity; in
due season you will learn to pray.

— Rev. Andrew Murray

A nd let us consider one another
to provoke unto love and to
good works.

— *Hebrews 10:24*

Studies show that good works like charity are "contagious" in social groups. People who know their friends or neighbors are giving are more likely to give themselves. We may feel more comfortable volunteering if a friend or loved one will be there with us. In turn, these shared acts help to foster our love for neighbors and community.

W e are not really apart, for you can touch God direct by prayer, and so can I.

— Mary Slessor

B lessed is the man that trusteth in the Lord, and whose hope the Lord is.

— Jeremiah 17:7

Living in difficult times requires us to maintain a positive, hopeful attitude about the future. Having hope is vital for our mental, physical, and spiritual health. Lord, help me move into the future with a steadfast spirit, looking forward in faith and hope and trusting in the promises you have made to your people.

B ecause prayer is the greatest power in the world; because it can alter the will of God towards us, because it can move the hand of the omnipotent God and is thus endued with His omnipotence, our prayers as we gather in the sanctuaries are no longer the submission of quietism, but a wrestling with God — the crying of a soul as in agony for victory based on the triumph of righteousness.

— Norman Maclean

B lessed are the pure in heart: for they shall see God.

— Matthew 5:8

Lord, my youngest daughter is the sweetest person I've ever met. Sometimes I can't believe she belongs to us. She loves every person and thing down to ladybugs and daddy long legs, and she radiates goodness and loving-kindness wherever we go. I know that she'll grow up and change at least a little, but these beautiful early years are such a blessing. Please walk with me as I help her to protect her spirit as she learns about the world and finds her place in it. I know she will love you as I do and rely on you for strength and courage to be herself.

The first thing the Lord teaches His disciples is that they must have a secret place for prayer; every one must have some solitary spot where he can be alone with his God. Every teacher must have a schoolroom.

— Henry Altemus

Put them in mind to be subject to principalities and powers, to obey magistrates, to be ready to every good work, to speak evil of no man, to be no brawlers, but gentle, shewing all meekness unto all men.

— *Titus 3:1–2*

What more can I say, dear God, than I've said since before my beloved newly adult child was born? Watch over and visit this young person with your presence. I'm better at roots than wings. Remind me that nothing can separate us from one another or your love. Help me be there for my children as you are for me, companion God. Go with this child today. I mustn't follow too closely, and I can't yet judge my distance.

He who believes in the efficacy of his father's or mother's prayers lives a nobler life than the skeptic.

—*Russell H. Conwell*

*A*nd this is life eternal, that they might know thee the only true God, and Jesus Christ, whom thou hast sent.

— John 17:3

Once I talked with a friend who always said he was a Christian. "Do you believe in Jesus Christ Almighty as your lord and savior?" I said. He said he didn't, but that he'd been raised a Christian and still felt like he was one. But Lord, I know that isn't good enough. You sent your son to earth that we might all be saved from our sins. We must love one another but we must also believe in you and the sacrifice you made, the son you gave, to give us a chance to follow you for eternity. Please help my friend to find you, and help me to keep you in my heart. Amen.

S cripture calls us to pray for many
things: for all saints; for all men;
for kings and all rulers; for all who are
in adversity; for the sending forth of
labourers; for those who labour in the
gospel; for all converts; for believers who
have fallen into sin; for one another in
our own immediate circles. The Scripture
calls to prayer demand a large heart,
taking in all saints, and all men, and
all needs.

— Rev. Andrew Murray

S *eeing ye have purified your souls in obeying the truth through the Spirit unto unfeigned love of the brethren, see that ye love one another with a pure heart fervently.*

— 1 Peter 1:22

Welcome to our party, Lord of water-into-wine feastings. Stand with us as we honor our special loved ones on this great occasion. Be with us, their friends and family, as we share a meal, a memory, and a toast to each other. Be present at their daily table as you are with them around this festive banquet now. On every occasion, Lord, you are the true reason for celebration.

P rayer had been her solace and
strength during all these days
and nights, and now with passionate
entreaty she beseeched God for guidance
and help in the struggle that was to
come. When she rose from her knees her
fear had vanished, and she was tranquil
and confident. For God was good, and
He was leading her, and that was perfect
happiness.

— William Pringle Livingstone

F or whosoever will save his life shall lose it; but whosoever shall lose his life for my sake and the gospel's, the same shall save it. For what shall it profit a man, if he shall gain the whole world, and lose his own soul?

— Mark 8:35-36

We've all heard stories of wealthy people who left their riches to charity, surprising everyone. Often the real story is how their children try to overturn these wills, claiming that only a person not in his right mind could give away so much. But Mark tells us plainly that it is only those in their right minds who give it all away. To gently tread in the footsteps of Christ we must leave our heaviest possessions and be ready to carry others who may not know the way.

E ven when we do not remember it, there is One, the Beginner and Finisher of faith and prayer, who watches over our praying, and sees to it that in all who trust Him for it their education in the school of prayer shall be carried on to perfection.

— Henry Altemus

T he mistake of Christians is in not praying over little things. Consult God about everything. Expect His counsel, His guidance, His care, His provision, His deliverance, His blessing, in everything.

— D.W. Whittle

And Jesus called a little child unto him, and set him in the midst of them, And said, Verily I say unto you, Except ye be converted, and become as little children, ye shall not enter into the kingdom of heaven. Whosoever therefore shall humble himself as this little child, the same is greatest in the kingdom of heaven.

— Matthew 18:2–4

✠ ✠ ✠

Today I kicked off my "grown-up" shoes and played barefoot in the yard. So much of life is complex and demanding but the greatest pleasures and fulfillments can be simple: a warm, sunny day; a sound night's sleep; a child's hand to hold while we watch cartoons together. Lord, your love for me is simple and powerful, and I am humbled by its magnitude.

Help me, O Lord my God: O save me according to thy mercy: That they may know that this is thy hand; that thou, Lord, hast done it.

— *Psalms 109:26–27*

Some people say adult life is like high school repeated, with all the cliques, scheming, and backstabbing you could ask for. But our relationship with God should make us bigger and better. Living well is the best payback, as they say.

When we pray for all saints, or for missions in general, it is difficult to know when or how our prayer is answered, or whether our prayer has had any part in bringing the answer. It is of extreme importance that we should prove that God hears us, and to this end take note of what answers we look for, and when they come.

— Rev. Andrew Murray

It is Jesus, praying Himself, who teaches to pray. He knows what prayer is. He learned it amid the trials and tears of His earthly life.

— Henry Altemus

*L*ooking *unto Jesus the author and finisher of our faith; who for the joy that was set before him endured the cross, despising the shame, and is set down at the right hand of the throne of God.*

— Hebrews 12:2

Reflect on the idea of a "finisher," like the keystone in an archway. Without the keystone, the arch collapses, no matter how the other stones are arranged.

One day, two boys came in, and we had everything to clothe them except a jacket for one of them. The matron, a very godly woman, said, "We must just pray that God will send what is needed," and we prayed that He would. That night a large [parcel] of clothing came, and in it was a jacket that fitted the boy as if it had been made for him. That was a small thing, of course, but if you don't see God in the gift of a pair of stockings you won't see Him in a gift of $10,000.

— William Quarrier

T rusteth in God, and continueth in supplications and prayers night and day.

— *1 Timothy 5:5*

✢ ✢ ✢

Throughout the Bible we see these exhortations to both faith and works. In 1 Timothy 5 we learn to expect this of our fellow believers and to let social support bring us all closer to God. Who bolsters your faith?

B eloved, if God so loved us, we ought also to love one another.

— 1 John 4:11

Please join us, Lord, to honor the grandparents who tended us so well. Pause with us as we play again in the dusty lanes of childhood at Grandma and Grandpa's house. Bless these larger-than-life companions who helped us bridge home and away, childhood and maturity. In their footsteps, we made the journey. Thank you for such a heritage. We express our gratitude to you.

The religious soul must believe in a real Divine Being. One condition necessary to successful prayer is a fixed belief in the Maker of all things.

— Russell H. Conwell

Is any among you afflicted? let him pray. Is any merry? let him sing psalms.

— James 5:13

A Christian minister once said to me: "Is it possible that the great God of the universe, the Maker and Ruler of mankind, could or would, as you would make out, take interest in such a trifle as the trimming of a hat! To me it is preposterous!" Yet did not our Lord Jesus Christ say: "The very hairs of your head are all numbered"; and "not one sparrow is forgotten before God"; and again, "Your heavenly Father knoweth what ye have need of before ye ask him"? It is true that "There is nothing too great for God's power"; and it is just as true that "There is nothing too small for his love!"

— Rosalind Goforth

At that day ye shall ask in my name: and I say not unto you, that I will pray the Father for you.

— *John 16:26*

Lord, increase the strength of our bonds of love so that we might bear witness to your love in our community. Give us the desire to offer hospitality at every opportunity. And throughout all our days together, may this family learn to worship better and better, seeing all you have so graciously given us.

The use of prayer is to bring us into communion with God, for the growth of the spiritual life, that is ours by faith in Christ Jesus. To leave it upon any lower plane than this, is to rob it of its highest functions and to paralyze it of lasting power for good in any direction. The promises of God are conditioned upon our being in this state of heart toward God.

— D.W. Whittle

I will therefore that men pray every where, lifting up holy hands, without wrath and doubting.

— 1 Timothy 2:8

O Lord, hear my prayer for all who are in trouble this day. Comfort those who are facing the loss of a loved one. Let your hope fill their hearts as they recall all your past faithfulness. Let them be assured that you can take care of every need, no matter how large or small. Heal those who are suffering pain and illness. Let them find rest and calm as they seek to make the idle moments pass more quickly. May they find joy in just one moment at a time. And may that be enough for now. In all these ways I ask your blessing upon those in trouble.

I am upheld and sustained by the good wishes and prayers of God's people. No one is more deeply than myself aware that without His favor our highest wisdom is but as foolishness and that our most strenuous efforts would avail nothing in the shadow of His displeasure. I am conscious of no desire for my country's welfare that is not in consonance with His will, and of no plan upon which we may not ask His blessing.

— Abraham Lincoln

*A*fter two days will he revive us: in the third day he will raise us up, and we shall live in his sight.

— Hosea 6:2

Dear God, complaints sometimes come first before I can feel free to love you. Sometimes you seem distant and unreasonable, uncaring. Help me understand why life can be so hurtful and hard. Hear my complaints and, in the spirit of compassion, show me how to move through pain to rebirth.

Desired ends are gained by prayer which cannot be gained by any other method. The daily experiences of devout persons establish that fact conclusively. The reasons and the methods which produce the results seem hidden, and they often bewilder the investigator. God's thoughts are far above our thoughts. But we can trust our daily experience far enough to retain our confidence in the potency of prayer. It is, therefore, a profitable and comforting study.

— Russell H. Conwell

M editate upon these things; give thyself wholly to them; that thy profiting may appear to all. Take heed unto thyself, and unto the doctrine; continue in them: for in doing this thou shalt both save thyself, and them that hear thee.

— 1 Timothy 4:15–16

✢ ✢ ✢

Blessed are you who know how to celebrate the goodness of life. Blessed because you choose to see the grace above and beyond the pain. Blessed because you see a potential friend in every stranger you meet. Blessed because you know the darkest clouds have brilliant silver linings. And most blessed because: All you ever knew of the half-empty glass was that it was almost full.

Every truly converted man knows from this experience that God answers prayer. His life is a life of prayer, and grows more and more to be a life of almost unconscious dependence upon God, as he becomes fixed in the habit of prayer. This, and it is the purpose of God, is the result secured by prayer. With this in view, it will not be so much what we expect to get by praying, as a consciousness of coming into closer relations to God, the giver of all, in our prayers, that will give us true joy.

— D.W. Whittle

I will not leave you comfortless: I will come to you.

— John 14:18

Lord, the infrequent visit with a distant friend is like reading a good book—at the end of each I feel the loneliness and pain of parting, combined with the satisfaction of time well spent. Please watch over my friends during their travels and keep them close to you.

Think of God in His infinite majesty, His altogether incomprehensible glory, His unapproachable holiness, sitting on a throne of grace, waiting to be gracious, inviting, encouraging you to pray with His promise: "Call upon Me, and I will answer thee."

— Rev. Andrew Murray

The enthusiast bubbles up with the Spirit of God within him, and it pours forth from him like a fountain. The word prophecy is misunderstood. Many suppose that it is limited to mere prediction; that is but the lesser portion of prophecy. The greater work is to reveal God. Every true religious enthusiast is a prophet.

— Walt Whitman

Hear me when I call, O God of my righteousness: thou hast enlarged me when I was in distress; have mercy upon me, and hear my prayer.

— Psalms 4:1

Like a speed bump in the drive-through, a decision lies in our path, placed there by God to remind us hope is a choice. Choosing to live as people of hope is not to diminish or belittle pain and suffering or lie about evil's reality. Rather it is to cling to God's promise that he will make all things new.

When we have illustrations before our eyes of God's care for his children, and His response to their faith, even in the minutest things, we understand the meaning of His promises and the reality of His providences.

— D.W. Whittle

The reports of the answers to prayer so often use the words "happened to think." The great list of mysterious impulses and intuitions which were noticed in those interesting seasons of prayer could not have been all accidental nor could they be classed under the natural laws of cause and effect.

— Russell H. Conwell

F or verily I say unto you, That whosoever shall say unto this mountain, Be thou removed, and be thou cast into the sea; and shall not doubt in his heart, but shall believe that those things which he saith shall come to pass; he shall have whatsoever he saith.

— Mark 11:23

When trouble strikes, we're restored by the smallest gestures from God's ambassadors: friends, random kindnesses, shared pain and support, even a stranger's outstretched hand. And we get the message: God cares.

A widow prayed for some leadership in the sale of some wild land in Louisiana. Her relatives urged her to let it go, as the "taxes will soon eat it all." But the unexpected payment of a debt due her led her to feel that, as she had been temporarily provided for, she would wait. In about seven weeks she read in a paper that a company had struck oil on the next section to her estate.

— Russell H. Conwell

H e that loveth not knoweth not God; for God is love. In this was manifested the love of God toward us, because that God sent his only begotten Son into the world, that we might live through him.

— 1 John 4:8–9

Never let our need overshadow our recognition of the needs of others. Ground us in empathy. Commission our sympathy. Urge us to offer comforting hands and understanding hearts. And in so doing, show us how easing the pain of others eases our own.

G ive us help from trouble: for vain is the help of man.

— *Psalms 108:12*

Dear Lord, I am blessed to have such good friends in my life, friends who share my sadness and my joy, my pain and my excitement, and who are always there for me when I need them. Just as I can lean on you for anything, Lord, I know you have given me these angels on earth who I can lean on as well. The love of these wonderful people fills my soul. I could not imagine living without them. May I always do for them what they have done for me.

A short time since I asked a dear friend whose writings have reached and inspired multitudes throughout the Christian world: "How did you do it?" Softly, with deep reverence in look and tone, she replied: "It has been done all in and through prayer!" With deepest gratitude and praise to our ever faithful God, I too can testify that any little service I have been able to do has been done by his grace in answer to prayer.

— Rosalind Goforth

W e give thanks to God always for you all, making mention of you in our prayers.

— 1 Thessalonians 1:2

Expressing gratitude is a simple way to feel more connected: to our loved ones, to our daily lives, and to God. Taking time to pray for your own "you all" is good for everyone involved.

A man may pray night and day, and yet deceive himself; but no man can be assured of his sincerity who does not pray. Prayer is faith passing into act; a union of the will and the intellect realising in an intellectual act. It is the whole man that prays. Less than this is wishing, or lip-work; a charm or a mummery. Pray always, says the apostle: that is, have the habit of prayer, turning your thoughts into acts by connecting them with the idea of the redeeming God, and even so reconverting your actions into thoughts.

— Samuel Taylor Coleridge

B ehold, I am the Lord, the God of all flesh: is there any thing too hard for me?

— *Jeremiah 32:27*

Prayer can move mountains, they say. But I've never seen a mountain budge...except in an earthquake or volcanic eruption. The results of persistent prayer can have the same earth-shaking, explosive results.

Y e ask, and receive not, because ye ask amiss, that ye may consume it upon your lusts.

— James 4:3

When James writes of "lusts," he seems to include all earthly delights. What we ask of God should in turn help us to serve and honor God, and our basic needs fall into that category. Don't be afraid to ask!

*A*s every man hath received the gift, even so minister the same one to another, as good stewards of the manifold grace of God.

— 1 Peter 4:10

Being a friend means that you need to reach out. Is there someone you can think of who needs to know that you are there for them— that you are a friend who cares? Pray for the spirit of friendship to so light up your life that you'll radiate this brightness to someone who needs you.

*A*nd he said unto them, When ye pray, say, Our Father which art in heaven, Hallowed be thy name. Thy kingdom come. Thy will be done, as in heaven, so in earth.

— Luke 11:2

Scooting over to make room, God of daily bread, the kids and I greet you over our peanut butter and jelly lunch. Through simple graces and verses to bless childhood fare and bedtime prayers to offer you the day, I'm honored to introduce you to my child.

Now, indeed, if never before, the heavens declared the glory of God. It was to the full sky of the Bible, of Arabia, of the prophets, and of the oldest poems.

— Walt Whitman

The bands that mothers and sisters weave by prayer and precept are the strongest in the world.

— Mary Slessor

S ing and rejoice, O daughter of Zion: for, lo, I come, and I will dwell in the midst of thee, saith the Lord.

— Zechariah 2:10

I f seamen have been forced to be scientific, they have been equally forced to be religious. They that go down to the sea in ships see both the works of the Lord, and also His wonders in the deep. They see God's works, regular, orderly, the same year by year, voyage by voyage, and tide by tide; and they learn the laws of them, and are so far safe. But they also see God's wonders. With all their knowledge, they have still plenty of ignorance; and therefore, with all their science, they have still room for religion.

— Charles Kingsley

Two lovers, separated far and praying long for each other, is an exhibition of the truest, sweetest love. It is, also, the best test of God's disposition to heed the requests of his children. No prayer for another can be felt to be effective which is not inspired more or less by real love.

— Russell H. Conwell

O lord, thou hast searched me, and known me.

— *Psalms 139:1*

God, it's that time again, when my children are off to school; when my house becomes a little less noisy and my life becomes a little less hectic. I will miss them, but I will also cherish this time for me. Time to work on my own life, time to follow my own dreams, time to listen to the prompting of my own inner voice. As the days grow shorter outside, let me make use of my time in the highest and best ways. Let me be me for a while, until they all come back home again. Amen!

While we ordinarily first bring our own needs to God in prayer, and then think of what belongs to God and His interests, the Master reverses the order. In true worship the Father must be first, must be all. The sooner I learn to forget myself in the desire that He may be glorified, the richer will the blessing be that prayer will bring to myself. No one ever loses by what he sacrifices for the Father.

— Henry Altemus

I will praise thee with my whole heart: before the gods will I sing praise unto thee.

— *Psalms 138:1*

Inspired by you, O God, I wisely invest in the future by deciding to chase kites on spring days, to chase balls on playgrounds, and to chase laughter rising from a baby's lips like bubbles on the wind rather than to chase dust bunnies beneath beds! Amen.

T he firmament of Bible story blazes with answers to prayer, from the days when Elijah unlocked the heavens on to the days when the petitions in the house of John Mark unlocked the dungeon, and brought liberated Peter into their presence. The whole field of providential history is covered with answered prayers as thickly as bright-eyed daisies cover our Western prairies. Find thy happiness in pleasing God, and sooner or later He will surely grant thee the desires of thy heart.

— Theodore L. Cuyler, D.D.

A s for me, this is my covenant with them, saith the Lord; My spirit that is upon thee, and my words which I have put in thy mouth, shall not depart out of thy mouth, nor out of the mouth of thy seed, nor out of the mouth of thy seed's seed, saith the Lord, from henceforth and for ever.

— *Isaiah 59:21*

Dear God, as I rise each day, give me the strength, courage, and patience to do the best I can for my family. All through the day, guide me with your grace and divine direction into right action and right decision. And when the day is done and it is time for me to rest my weary mind and body, take the burden of my troubles from me so that I can sleep. Watch over me and mine throughout the night, and

when it is time to arise to a new day, be there
for me all over again. Amen.

I do not make that great distinction between the hand of God and natural law,
and I have no wish to induce you to pray
by an accumulation of facts—to commend
to you the mighty secret by showing that it
would be profitable to you, a kind of Alad-
din's lamp for fulfilling wayward desires.
　　　　　　　　　— R.F. Horton, M.A., D.D.

But *without faith it is impossible to please him: for he that cometh to God must believe that he is, and that he is a rewarder of them that diligently seek him.*

— Hebrews 11:6

Bless me with the kind heart of a peacemaker and a builder's sturdy hand, Lord, for these are mean-spirited, litigious times when we tear down with words and weapons first and ask questions later. Help me take every opportunity to compliment, praise, and applaud as I rebuild peace.

H ere on earth Christ as man came to reveal what prayer is. To pray in the Name of Christ we must pray as He prayed on earth; as He taught us to pray; in union with Him, as He now prays in heaven.

— Rev. Andrew Murray

*A*nd this is the confidence that we have in him, that, if we ask any thing according to his will, he heareth us: And if we know that he hear us, whatsoever we ask, we know that we have the petitions that we desired of him.

— 1 John 5:14–15

Are there graces for lettuce, Lord? And low-fat, no-fat, meat-free, fun-free meals? I need you to send me words for blessing this paltry meal, for it's hard to feel grateful for these skimpy portions when all I think of are the foods not on my plate. Help me change that thought, to make peace with choosing not to eat them, for I need help in becoming the healthier person I want to be. Hold up for me a mirror of the new creation you see me becoming, for I need a companion at this table. "Lettuce pray!" Amen.

S t. Patrick loved the Irish people; and he was continually praying that God would bestow favours on them. And his prayers were answered; for, after the Apostolic times, there never were more devoted or more successful missionaries than those who preached the Gospel in Ireland, and there never were people who received the Faith more readily than the Irish, or who practised it after their conversion with more piety and earnestness.

— P. W. Joyce

Hitherto have ye asked nothing in my name: ask, and ye shall receive, that your joy may be full.

— John 16:24

Everything in my life lately seems to be going wrong. People are uncaring. Things I've worked hard for don't seem to be coming to fruition. Everyone needs my time and attention and I feel so tired and overwhelmed and stressed. I ask today in prayer for peace, for serenity. I don't ask for a removal of my problems, but for the power and fortitude to deal with them as they arise from a place of calm and stillness within. I know that you can provide me that kind of amazing, unerring peace, God. Be the rock upon which I can take comfort and rest when the world spins out of control all around me. Be my peace everlasting, dear God.

P rayer can do anything; let us try its power.

— Mary Slessor

T hou hast commanded us to keep thy precepts diligently. O that my ways were directed to keep thy statutes! Then shall I not be ashamed, when I have respect unto all thy commandments.

— Psalms 119:4–6

✛ ✛ ✛

In your wisdom, you designed us to reject the word "don't." Like all your children, mine do better with "do" words. Do love, share, work, tend, tolerate, obey, forgive. Help me say "do" as often as I can. Let me be a positive example of your vision.

N ow mine eyes shall be open, and mine ears attent unto the prayer that is made in this place.

— 2 Chronicles 7:15

We sit around the table, my family and I, and celebrate the blessings God has given us. Blessings of loved ones, of good food, and of the shared bounty of the earth. Blessings of a warm, happy home filled with laughter and joy. Blessings of times spent together, of achievements and successes. Blessings of lessons we've learned, of silver linings surrounding every dark cloud, and of rainbows following every dreary shower. But mostly we celebrate our faith; in ourselves, in each other, and in God. Faith is the foundation of our strength, the bedrock of our joy.

T he prayerful soul must be sure that "God is," and that he heeds the call of his children.

— Russell H. Conwell

L et us stir up the slumbering gift that is lying unused, and seek to gather and train and band together as many as we can.

— Rev. Andrew Murray

And I will make of thee a great nation, and I will bless thee, and make thy name great; and thou shalt be a blessing: And I will bless them that bless thee, and curse him that curseth thee: and in thee shall all families of the earth be blessed.

— Genesis 12:2–3

Lord, the only blessing I ask for these days is to restore my body and mind to wellness. When I am healthy and strong, everything else seems easier and I have the fortitude to handle challenges that come my way. Bless me with good health and vitality, and help me treat my body right and avoid stress when I can.

At first sight it might appear as if this thought made prayer less needful: God knows far better than we what we need. But as we get a deeper insight into what prayer really is, this truth will help much to strengthen our faith. It will teach us that we do not need, as the heathen, with the multitude and urgency of our words, to compel an unwilling God to listen to us.

— Henry Altemus

And when they heard that, they lifted up their voice to God with one accord, and said, Lord, thou art God, which hast made heaven, and earth, and the sea, and all that in them is.

— Acts 4:24

Thank you for the bright colors of summer! I look around and see the sun in the sky, the clear moon in the night, the brilliance of the flowers and the trees. Thank you, Lord, for blessing me with color in my life. I know that even the darkest, dreariest days cannot last for-ever, just as the memory of winter fades during summer's glory.